First published in 1998 by

Wilbek & Lewbar
90 Victoria Road, Devizes
Wiltshire, SN10 1EU

Collection by   Rod Priddle
Editor   Bob Wilson
Illustrations   Ted Sibbick
Design & Layout   Emma Greenland

Printed in Great Britain

ISBN 1 901284 12 3

© Copyright 1998

Foreword

It is a unique quality of human nature which, in the midst of the cruelty, tragedy, bloodiness and hatred of war, allows sensitivity to thrive. There can be few better examples of this human quality than the poetry and prose which has been written in the quieter moments after a day's conflict or after victory has been won.

In this very moving book, Rod Priddle allows the reader insight to the thoughts and feelings of those fighting the war in the air and, as important, the anguish of those left behind and not knowing whether they will ever see their loved ones again. 'Wings of the BRAVE' will be a comfort and insight for all those who have flown fighting machines or have been close to those who have done so.

We at the Royal Air Force Benevolent Fund feel privileged to receive the royalties from this excellent book and our thanks go to Rod Priddle for his kindness. Put simply, the Fund has existed for 80 years to bring relief from hardship to those who have served in the RAF and its associated services. Any rank, male or female, ground personnel or aircrew, and their families can apply to the Fund for help and this eligibility lasts for life. The royalties from this book will help us continue our invaluable welfare work.

Thank you for buying 'Wings of the BRAVE';
I know you will enjoy reading it.

By **Air Commodore C H Reineck OBE,**
    Director Appeals,
    RAF Benevolent Fund

This book is dedicated to
Uncle Bill
*Sergeant M.P.R. Del Rosso (1336667)
Pilot - No. 502 (Ulster) Squadron
Coastal Command - St. Eval - 1942/43*

Introduction

The poems in this book were written mainly by those who took part in the various theatres of air warfare around the world. It describes their experiences, their thoughts and fears, the aircraft they flew, the enemy they rarely saw, the airfields they called home and the colleagues who were never to come home.

Some of the poetry was written to amuse, or as a dedication to a friend or to an aircraft type, to which lives had been entrusted and the trust rewarded by a safe return or perhaps the completion of a successful tour of operations. Some contributions are very poignant, producing a shiver down the spine or making the hairs on the back of the neck stand on end. Different poems will affect people's feelings in different ways, but surely the now famous 'High Flight' by the American, Pilot Officer John Magee, must be one of the most emotive pieces of poetry written during World War 2. The passage was paraphrased by the President of the United States of America, Ronald Reagan, at the service for the crew members who died during the launch of the Challenger space craft at Cape Canaveral on the 29th January 1986. The proud words of 'Lie in the Dark and Listen' from the Collected Lyrics of Noel Coward exemplify all that Bomber Command stood for during its nightly raids over Europe.

This poetry forms part of a collection made over a number of years for my own pleasure. Later in the year it is the intention to issue later a further selection of poems associated entirely with Bomber Command and to follow that with a selection covering various aspects of military flying. The culmination will be a hard backed omnibus edition. If these works act to remind the reader of the young people from all corners of the globe who came together to serve this nation during the dark days of war, with so many paying the ultimate price, then I ask no more.

My own contribution will be to donate the royalties from the sale of this book to the Royal Air Force Benevolent Fund in the knowledge that it will assist the quality of life of some of the airmen and women and their relative's in a time of possible need.

Contents

Foreword	page 2
Introduction	page 4
Contents	page 6
Flight	page 7
High Flight	page 9
Ad Astra	page 11
The Fringe Of Glory, 1940	page 12
Luna Habitabilis	page 13
Commonplace, 1943	page 14
Fighter Pilot's Wife	page 15
View From The Train	page 16
Beaten Up On The Circuit	page 17
After Battle	page 19
February 25th, 1943	page 21
The Last Scramble	page 23
Per Ardua	page 25
Biggin Hill, July 1947	page 26
Ubiquitous Coastal	page 27
To An Absent Friend	page 29
The Flying Instructors Lament	page 30
Passing Of A Hurricane	page 31
Hurricane, 1940	page 32
We, The Bombers	page 33
Short Prayer	page 35
Tribute To A Lanc	page 36
Showpiece - Lancaster	page 37
Lie In The Dark and Listen	page 39
Acknowledgments	page 41
Information	page 43

Flight

How can they know that joy to be alive
Who have not flown?
To loop and spin and roll and climb and dive,
The very sky one's own,
The surge of power while engines race,
The sting of speed,
The rude winds' buffet on one's face,
To live indeed.

How can they know the grandeur of the sky
The earth below,
The restless sea, and waves that break and die
With ceaseless ebb and flow;
The morning sun on drifting clouds
And rolling downs -
And valley mist that shrouds
The chimneyed towns?

So long has puny man to earth been chained
Who now is free,
And with the conquest of the air has gained
A glorious liberty.
How splendid is this gift He gave
On high to roam,
The sun a friend, the earth a slave,
The heavens home.

Flight Cadet Brian P. Young - RAF
RAF Cranwell - 1938

Brian Young, *a South African by birth, entered RAF Cranwell where he was awarded the Sword of Honour. He was commissioned on the 30th July 1938 and went on to join No. 615 Squadron as a Pilot Officer flying Hurricane I's. He was shot down on the 13th May 1940 over France and after a long period of medical treatment he returned to operational duties in 1942 as a Flight Commander with No.422 (RCAF) Squadron of Coastal Command. He eventually attained the rank of Air Vice Marshal on the 1st January 1968. AVM Brian Young CB, CBE retired on the 5th May 1973.*

High Flight

Oh! I have slipped the surly bonds of Earth
And danced the skies on laughter-silvered wings;
Sunward I've climbed, and joined the tumbling mirth
Of sun-split clouds and done a hundred things
You have not dreamed of, wheeled and soared and swung
High in sunlit silence, Hov'ring there,
I've chased the shouting wind along, and flung
My eager craft through footless halls of air...
Up, up the long, delirious, burning blue
I've topped the wind-swept heights with easy grace,
Where never lark, or even eagle flew -
And, while with silent, lifting mind I've trod
The high untrespassed sanctity of space,
Put out my hand and touched the face of God.

Pilot Officer John Gillespie Magee, Jnr. RCAF - No.412 Sq.
Summer 1941

by kind permission of This England magazine.

John Magee was an American citizen, born in Shanghai and educated at Rugby in England. He joined the Royal Canadian Air Force in the summer of 1940. It was whilst he was attending his Operational Training Unit at Llandow in South Wales in the summer of 1941 that he wrote "High Flight" and it was about ten days prior to his first operational posting in September 1941, with RCAF No. 412 (Falcon) Squadron at RAF Digby where he flew the Spitfire IIa.

The Squadron moved to RAF Wellingore on the 20th October 1941, flying Spitfire Vb.'s and it was shortly after this on the 8th November that John Magee was in action. This took place over France when his Squadron on this occasion were operating from RAF West Malling with two other Squadrons, providing cover for a raid by Blenheim bombers on the Locomotive Works at Lille. Whilst he fired his guns he was unable to claim any damage to the enemy Me. 109's and Focke-Wolf 190's that engaged them. It was just over a month later, on the 11th December, that John Magee was killed at the age of 19 years, when flying through a bank of cloud, his Spitfire AD291 collided with an Airspeed Oxford piloted by a student from RAF Cranwell which at that time was a Service Flying Training School. The port wing of the Spitfire broke off and the engine fell out. It spun out of control and by the time John Magee had released himself from the cockpit, he was too low for his parachute to deploy. The Spitfire crashed in a field between Wellingore and Cranwell. The pilot of the Oxford was also killed and John Magee was buried, following a service funeral, at the village church of Scopwick near Digby. His headstone includes the first and last lines from 'High Flight'.

Ad Astra

I took my leave of the earth and men,
And soared aloft to the lonely sky,
Thro' the gathering dark, to the silent stars,
And the whisper of Angels passing by.

I heard the beat of the Angels wings,
In the silent watch of the starlit night.
I felt His touch, and I heard His voice.
I, Man, communed with the Infinite.

Far below lies a burnt out wreck,
Soft, the strains of bugles sound.
The Ensign flutters a last salute
As another pilot is laid to ground.

Men are sighing, and women weep.
Ah! foolish friends, do not grieve for me,
For I heard God call in the silent night,
And flew on, into Eternity.

SRN Molly Corbally - Territorial Army Nursing Service

Molly Corbally joined the Service in January 1940. She served four years in the 19th General Field Hospital, Bitter Lakes on the Suez Canal in Egypt.

The Fringe Of Glory, 1940

I have touched the fringe of glory
and flown the high blue sky,
I was there, when men of courage
had said that they - and I -
Could meet the storm that threatened,
oppose it and deny.

Oh, how they flew, outnumbered,
and fiercely stemmed the tide.
I knew those men of courage
and watched them as they died.

They're gone, but not forgotten
and bravely played their part.
The foe who would destroy us
had met the Lion-heart.

And now, in dimming memory,
yet overwhelming pride
I know that I was honoured
to be there at their side.

I still look up, and listen,
and hear the Merlin's roar,
See vapour trails, criss-crossing,
of many years before.

And then I stand, and silence
succeeds the angry noise
Of men in mortal combat,
some hardly men, just boys.

For England, Mother England,
Another Crispin's Day
Look up, as I, and see them
and with me, truly say
They hold the Fringe of Glory
and God will them repay.

Squadron Leader Ronald W. Wallens DFC, RAF- No 41 & 277 Squadrons.

Luna Habitabilis *(The Moon is Inhabited)*

The time will come, when thou shalt lift thine eyes,
To watch a long drawn battle in the skies,
And aged peasants too amazed for words,
Stare at the Flying Fleet of Won'drous birds.
England, so long Mistress of the Sea
Where winds and waves confess her sovereignty
Her ancient triumphs yet on high shall bear
And reign, the Sovereign of the conquered air.

By Thomas Gray (1716-71)

This extract from a poem by Thomas Gray has been taken from the original Latin and freely translated. He wrote it between the 29th December 1736 and 17th March 1737. It is doubtful that it was formed with a picture in his mind of battling aircraft defending the skies over Britain during the dark days of 1940. The triumphant air of the verse however, appears most appropriate to those times and it is for this reason that it has been thought worthy of inclusion in this anthology.

Commonplace, 1943

Their engines beating an even rhythm,
(Men look up from their work at the sound)
Wing-tip to wing-tip, they fly in formation -
Thirty-six Spitfires outward bound.

Slim and yet sturdy, like well bred terriers,
Each independent yet part of the whole,
Fierce but dispassionate, steady yet eager,
Thirty-six Spits on offensive patrol.

Over the coast-line see them returning,
Skimming like wild fowl close to the ground.
Men glance upwards to watch them flying -
Thirty-five Spitfires homeward bound.

Rosemary Anne Sisson

Fighter Pilots Wife

Because, whatever we may say or do,
You and I
Will always have that vision clear of you
In the sky.

Because you, who are young and strong of limb
Will have no power
To avert your destiny so bright and grim
In that hour.

Because, through all our warm and casual mirth,
You and I
Can always see you flaming down to earth
Across the sky.

Rosemary Anne Sisson

View From The Train

When we stop just outside Warlingham, and I look across, I see
The Hurricanes of 253 (Kenley) , racing out towards the sea
Are there flowers on the embankment?
Is it snowing, sunny, wet?
The Hurricanes of 253 (Kenley), race out to intercept
If I live another sixty years, the view will always be
The Hurricanes of 253 (Kenley) racing out towards the sea.

Unknown

Beaten Up On The Circuit

There are breath taking scenes on Malta
When come Hurricanes hard pressed to land,
Grimly winging around the circuit
With grey Messerschmitt fighters on hand;
And the Hun gloats on planes short of fuel
Being flown with their Browning guns spent
Of ammunition while still airborne
At the point of inglorious descent.

Thus endangered, two Hurricanes bank
To evade 'One 0 Nines' as they dive,
Ere both pilots side - slip to lose height
Ever hoping their planes will survive
An approach with wingflaps and wheels down
And fish tailing to minimise speed,
As if gliding while trying to land-
Which at first glance appears to succeed.

But alas, a wing tip hits the ground!
And a Hurricane cartwheels to roll,
On its port wing, propeller and tail
'Til it lands in a bomb cratered hole.
Then the second plane flown in the style
Of a lassoed and bucking mustang
Overshoots 'til the pilot retracts
Landing wheels for a belly-flop prang.

Aircraft beaten up on the circuit
Make a Hurricane pilot despair,
Since few planes have a chance to escape
From such one sided aerial warfare,
On an island besieged and reduced
To a battered and bomb cratered base -
Where bold Messerschmitt pilots excel
In a five to one, Hurricane chase.

John Snook RAF
RAF Ta Kali, Malta - April 1942

John Snook was posted to the beleaguered island of Malta as a nineteen year old in 1941 and remained there until 1944. During that period he was mainly stationed on the heavily bombed airfields at Luqa and Ta Kali where he penned an account of his experiences in rhyme and verse. In 1992 to coincide with the 50th Anniversary Celebrations of Malta's survival from the Luftwaffe's onslaughts, the poems were published (with the blessing of the George Cross Island Association) as "Malta Siege Verse 1941/1942/1943" -Koons. ISBN 0-620-14677-X.

After leaving the Royal Air Force, John Snook taught in United Kingdom and South Africa High Schools before obtaining Colonial Territory appointments. They included Headmasterships, educational broadcasting commissions and international press correspondent assignments. He is the author of books relating to a wide variety of Southern African subjects and is an award winning poet.

After Battle

Many things we had forgotten, we who knew
The boundless unpossessive joy of living -
One to another giving -
When death had brushed our wingtips as we flew:

Who proudly soared to battle, when the span
From dawn to sunset was eternity,
And death's simplicity
Laid bare the naked living soul of man.

First, we forgot that war had not removed
From those at home the toil, the sweat, the tears
The hopes of earlier years;
War is the absence of the one beloved.

Their hearts were numb with sorrow, in the sense
Of others dying, which is death in life
More pitiless than strife;
War is the sense of age's impotence.

And lastly, we forgot the constancy
Of those that burned the lantern at the gate
And sat, content to wait;
Peace is the finding of fidelity.

Pilot Officer David Scott-Malden, DSO, DFC*,
RAF - Nos. 611/ 603 Squadrons.

David Scott-Malden served with No. 611 Squadron, followed by a posting to No. 603 (City of Edinburgh) Squadron on the 3rd October 1940. At this time he was based at RAF Hornchurch, flying Spitfires and was soon involved in combat. On the 12th October during a dog-fight over Kent, he accounted for an Me 109 which crashed on the Kent Downs. The German pilot, Oblt Buesgen of I /JG52 baled out and became a prisoner of war. David Scott-Malden was officially credited with a total of 5 enemy aircraft destroyed.

He remained with the RAF after the war, eventually attaining the rank of Air Vice Marshal on the 1st July 1965. He retired on the 25th September 1966. The poem 'After Battle' was written in 1946 and the words are penned with his fighter squadron experiences in mind.

February 25th 1943

I flew in the war so we'd all be free,
And this was my life until '43.
The battle had been won and time quickly rolled,
I grew to be a man, but didn't grow old.

I remember the day of the final scramble,
Life was a dice, a card, a gamble.
The race to my 'mount' for that last flight,
Excited, apprehensive, stomach so tight.

Riding the clouds, bathed in the sun,
Tranquillity at the end of a gun.
Seeking the enemy, from where will he come,
The R/T crackled, "Vector 120... Angels 21 "!

Through the gate we raced, following the skipper,
Were his thoughts of his wife and the birth of his nipper?
I heard first the noise, felt the searing fire,
Knew God was my companion, I had grown tired.

Am I floating to earth, is my face unmarked?
Have I served life well, upon which I embarked?
I'm at peace now, resting beneath this tree,
One life ends, another begins - February 25th 1943.

Rod Priddle

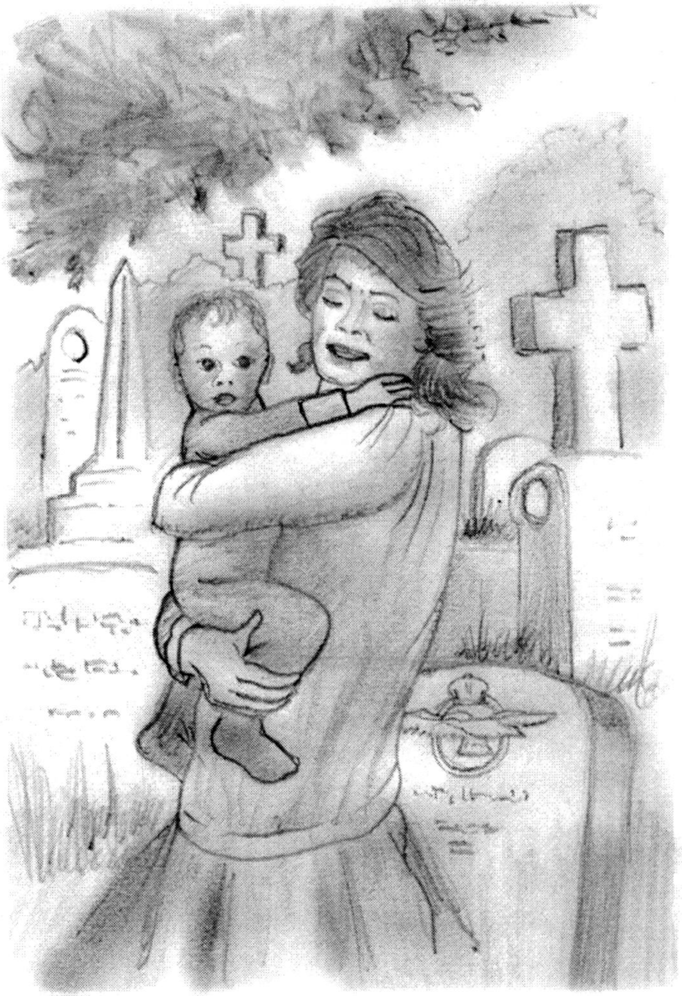

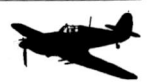

The Last Scramble

The time is not far distant, when I must face the door,
That opens on another world, which none have seen before.

The scene of dimming memory, the pilots, tense but calm,
Waiting, apprehensive, the Scramble bell's alarm.

The flush on boyish faces, the look from eager eyes,
To meet the fate awaited, in bullet ridden skies.

The waiting quickly ended, mad rushing for the door,
The strident cry "Get Airborne"! and mighty Merlin's roar.

Oh how I well remember my thoughts, and senses roused,
The sound and smell of Spitfires, machine and man espoused.

A thousand years it seems, since last I saw them fly,
To victory and glory, a wave, their last goodbye.

But what have I, who left behind, must face the final pain,
Of passing through that open door, that we may meet again.

Well, now I've made up my mind and when they ring the bell,
And cry, "come on young Wally", I'll scramble there like hell!

So, if you see a shadow. high climbing out of sight,
It's only me 'Green Leader', last scramble, and last flight!

Squadron Leader Ronald W. Wallens, DFC,
RAF - No 41 & 277 Squadrons

Squadron Leader 'Wally' Wallens joined the RAF on a short service commission in 1937 and as an Acting Pilot Officer he carried out training at Scone Aerodrome, EFTS Perth in Scotland followed by No 8FTS Montrose. His first posting after qualification in 1938 was to No 41 Fighter Squadron at Catterick, where initially he flew Fury II's until the squadron was reequipped with Spitfire I's. At the outbreak of war, No 41 Squadron were part of No. 13 Group. On the 19th October 1939 the squadron moved to Wick in Scotland but, returned to Catterick on the 25th October. During the following 12 months the squadron moved a number of times between Catterick and Homchurch which was in No. 12 Group. Whilst flying from Homchurch on the morning of the 8th August 1940 'Wally' destroyed 3 Messerschmitt BF 109's. That afternoon No 41 Squadron moved back to Catterick to rest. On the IIth August 'Wally' and his number 2 intercepted a Junkers JU 88 over Thirsk and shared in its destruction.

The squadron returned again to Homchurch on the 3rd September and two days later 'Wally' claimed a further BF 109 destroyed but, in the process was himself shot down at 15.40 hours in Spitfire X4021. Whilst negotiating a forced landing he sustained serious injury from the cannon and machine gun fire of another BF109. Following a lengthy period in hospital and convalescence 'Wally' was granted a limited non-operational flying category and was posted in the summer of 1941 to No. I ADF Hendon and Croydon, which he was later to command.

This unit was part of No II Group - Fighter Command. In the autumn of 1943 he was posted to No.277 Air Sea Rescue Squadron at Hawkinge flying Spitfire V's and the Walrus amphibian. In 1944 he became Commanding Officer and was also awarded his DFC. On the Ist August 1945 he was posted to Davidstow Moor in Cornwall, as a Senior Administrative Officer and later that year moved in the same post to nearby St.Eval. This was followed by a similar posting with No 6 OTU Coastal Command Kinloss. From this station he took his last in-service flight when he flew a Spitfire XVI and found himself over Scone Airfield in Perth where his career had started. 'Wally' left the RAF in 1949. He had been officially credited with 5 enemy aircraft destroyed.

Squadron Leader Wallens died aged 79 in 1996 and at his funeral service a reading was given by his daughter Karen of 'The Last Scramble' surely a most fitting tribute to one of the 'Few'

Per Ardua

They that have climbed the white mists of the morning;
They that have soared, before the world's awake,
To herald up their foe men to them, scorning
The thin dawn's rest their weary folk might take;

Some that have left other mouths to tell the story
Of high, blue battle, - quite young limbs that bled;
How they had thundered up the clouds to glory
Or fallen to an English field stained red;

Because my faltering feet would fail I find them
Laughing beside me, steadying the hand
That seeks their deadly courage - yet behind them
The cold light dies in that once brilliant land...

Do these, who help the quickened pulse run slowly,
Whose stern remembered image cools the brow -
Till the far dawn of Victory know only
Night's darkness, and Valhalla!s silence now?

(To those who gave their lives to England during the Battle of Britain and left such a shining example to us who follow, these lines are dedicated.)

Pilot Officer John Gillespie Magee, Jnr. RCAF - No. 412 Sq.

This was to be the last piece of poetry written by John Magee. He sent it to his parents just prior to his death with instructions that " If anyone should want this, please see that it is accurately copied, capitalized, and punctuated"

by kind permission of
This England magazine

Biggin Hill, July 1947

On Weald of Kent I watched once more
Again I heard that grumbling roar
Of fighter planes, yet none were near
And all around the sky was clear
Borne on the wind a whisper came
'Though men grow old, they stay the same'
And then I knew, unseen to eye
The ageless 'Few' were sweeping by.

Lord Harold Harington Balfour of Inchrye PC, MC*
Parliamentary Under-Secretary of State for Air 1938-44

Ubiquitous Coastal

From A.S.R. to P.R.U.
We did our best : we saw it through.
With bombs and rockets : Leigh-lights too.
With A.S.V. and weapons new,
We flew in Hudsons, Wimps and Boats.
We flew in sheepskins boots and coats.
We laid our mines where Group did wish,
While Torbeaus dropped their deadly 'fish'.
We struck at ships by night and day
In Blenheims, Mossies, Beauforts grey.
We scoured and harassed shipping lanes
In Libs and Cats and British planes.
We lost ten thousand crewmen true.
We did our best: we saw it through.

Squadron Leader Tony Spooner DSO,DFC,RAFVR.
Flight Commander - No. 53 Squadron

Tony Spooner joined the RAFVR in 1937. At the outbreak of war two years later was a civilian Pilot/Navigator Instructor under contract to the RAF at Sywell and later as an RAF officer at Blackpool with No.2 School of General Reconnaissance. In 1941 he flew a tour of operations with No.221 Squadron Coastal Command based at Limavady in Northern Ireland. He was the skipper of a Wellington VIII, hunting U-boats in the Atlantic. Later in 1941 he was posted to Malta as Officer Commanding Special Duties Flight. Later back in the United Kingdom, he was in charge of Wellington torpedo bomber training at Turnberry before becoming a Flight Commander with No. 53 Squadron based at Beaulieu and St. Eval, flying Liberators and completing a further 'Tour'. He was twice assigned duties alongside the Royal Navy. Post war he served as a Captain with B.O.A.C. Tony is now a successful military aviation author.

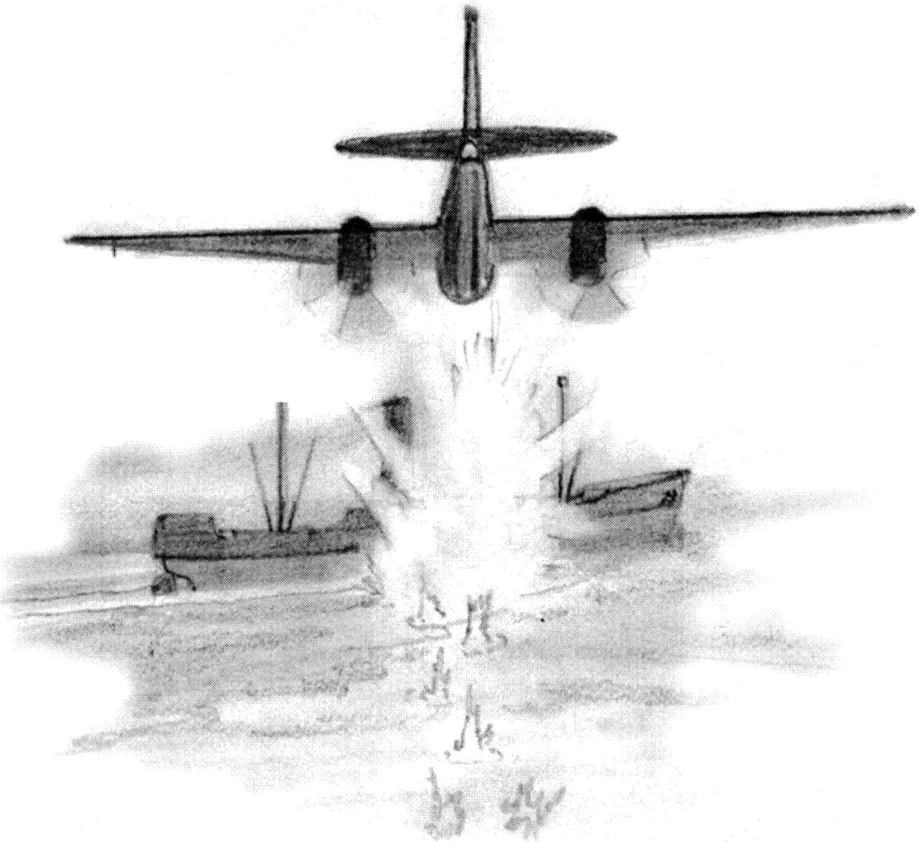

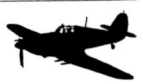

To An Absent Friend

Take down his coat,
Pack up his things.
The scribbled note,
The tunic with wings;
The books, cricket pads and bat,
And his beloved misshapen hat.

Auction his car,
Attend to his debts,
And then there are
His several pets,
The tortoise, collie dog and bird
Whose cheerful chirp is now unheard.

No more kissing
Or popsies thrilled;
He's reported 'Missing,
Believed Killed'.
He had no ribbons, won no fame,
We'll toast his memory just the same.

Squadron Leader Vernon Noble
RAF No.4 Group 1942

The Flying Instructor's Lament

"What did you do in the war daddy?
How did you help us win?"
"By teaching young fellows to fly, laddy
And how to get out of a spin".

Woe, alack and misery me!
I trundle around the sky,
And instead of machine gunning Nazis,
I'm teaching young hopefuls to fly.

So it's circuits and bumps from morning to noon,
And instrument flying till tea.
"Hold her off!"- Give her bank!" Put your undercart down!"
"You're skidding!"- "You're slipping!"- that's me.

And so soon as you have finished with one course,
Like a flash, up another one bobs.
And there's four more to try out the knobs!

But sometimes we read in the papers,
Of deeds that old pupils have done,
And we're proud to have seen their beginnings,
And shown them the way to the sun.

Unknown

Passing Of A Hurricane

As I walked down by Lewis Lane
To buy a roasting duck
There passed a broken Hurricane
Dismembered on a truck

Her wings lay folded at her side
A blackened, tattered pall,
And gaping bullet-holes supplied
The context of her fall.

The canvas discs which normally
Screen the eight gun-vents blast
Were shot away, brave proof that she
Fell firing to the last.

She went, and as I sought my roast
I thanked her for the day
When high above the Kentish coast
She dived into the fray.

And quite alone, no friends to see,
Fought twenty Messerschmitts
Who, having scored but one to three,
Repented of their blitz.

Then sudden, as I stopped and stood,
A roar came deep and strong-
A squadron of her sisterhood
Throating their battlesong.

Flight Lieutenant O.C. Chave - RAF - No.15 Sq.

Hurricane, 1940

Just twisted scrap thrown on a dump
Strips of wing and a Merlin sump
Old Fighter plane
Your flight is done
Your landings made and Victories won.

Gun barrels scorched and motors tired
Your masters fought as men inspired
Old Fighter plane
They trusted you
Who faithfully served the Gallant Few.

Casually now they fly around
Jet propelled at speed of sound
New Fighter planes
Fierce in your power
Spare a thought for those who had their hour.

Lord Harold Harington Balfour of Inchrye PC, MC & Bar
Under-Secretary of State for Air 1938-44

We, The Bombers

We have no graceful form, no flashing shape
To flicker, fish-like, in the dome of the sky;
No famous whine of motor, glint of light
Proclaims us to the earthling's ear or eye.
Darkly we go, unseen, by friends unsped,
Leaving the homely fields that are our own,
Up to the heights where sunset's early red
Changes to blackness. We are there alone.

No heat of battle warms our chilling blood;
No friendly soil beneath us if we fall;
Our only light the stars, whose fickle mood
Will lead them to desert us when we call.
Death down below or stealing through the dark
Awaits our coming with a silent grin.
Bellona's fireworks, curtained around our mark,
Form doors of fire through which we enter in.

Flame, smoke and noise surround us for a while;
A shuddered jerk - the load goes screaming down;
Cold hands and feet move levers for escape;
A chain of fire bespatters through the town.
Back to the darkness, friendly now, we speed
To count our wounds and set a course for home,
Speaking to Base, attentive to our need.
Watching for that far friendly line of foam.

Hour upon hour the long drawn journey runs;
Fighters and searchlights still our road proclaim.
Salt-eyed, we watch the heavens for the Huns,
Weary, we dodge the heaven-splitting flame.
Then, with no certain vict'ry to impart,
Out of the dawn we drop from frosty height,
Welcomed alone by those who saw us start
And watched and waited for us through the night.

P. Heath RAF
January 1942

This was written after he had been snubbed by a WAAF girl in the Mess Room of a Fighter Squadron. In her eyes, the role of the Fighter pilot was more glamorous.

Short Prayer

Almighty and all present Power,
Short is the prayer I make to Thee;
I do not ask, in battle hour,
For any shield to cover me.
The vast unalterable way
From which the stars do not depart
May not be turned aside to stay
The bullet flying to my heart.
I ask no help to strike my foe,
I seek no petty victory here;
The enemy I hate, I know
To Thee, 0 God, is also dear.
But this I pray, be at my side
When death is drawing through the sky.
Almighty God, who also died,
Teach me the way that I should die!

Flt.Sgt. Hugh Rowell Brodie RAAF-No 460 Sq

Hugh Brodie was based at Breighton in Yorkshire in No. I Group. He was killed on a raid over Essen in Germany on the 2nd June 1942. He was one of a 5 man crew of a Wellington IV. Z 1249(K) that took off at 23.30 hours but failed to return.

Tribute To A Lanc

In one brief moment on a summer's day,
You brought back memories of yesterday.
When you knew glory in those wartime skies,
But seemed outmoded in our children's eyes,
"It won the war"! I said to them with pride,
Its contributions cannot be denied.
Her crew were brave and dedicated men,
She flies as well as ever she did then.
Dear Lancaster, you great illustrious plane,
How wonderful to see you fly again!

Unknown

Showpiece - Lancaster

I dream of another time,
Of soaring wings, and slipstreams whine,
Of airscrew arcs, and engine drone,
And cloudy canyons I have known.

Once we were many, and we knew,
The love of thousands, our aircrew,
So many lovers, past recall,
Yet we were faithful to them all.

When towering columns split the night,
With brilliant beams of searching light,
There in just moments, we became,
Small insects, round a naked flame.

And with us then, our young men knew,
An eighth, unwanted, crewman flew,
He whispered, taunted, often near,
Unseen, but known, for he was Fear.

Time after time, we saw the cost,
To all who fought so well, yet lost,
For them a fiery plunge through space,
In another time, another place.

For you old lovers, youth has gone,
Relentless, time is moving on,
With arms outstretched, with measured pace,
To take you all in cold embrace.

Time has not marred my grim old frame,
To your fading eyes, I am the same,
Look well, all strangers, standing there,
For I am the mighty Lancaster.

Walter Scott - RAF Wireless Operator/Air-gunner - No 630 Squadron

This poem by Walter Scott relates to an old Lancaster Bomber that will never fly again but which has been placed on display in an air-museum.

Lie In The Dark And Listen

Lie in the dark and listen.
It's clear tonight, so they're flying high-
Hundreds of them, thousands perhaps,
Riding the icy moonlit sky-
Men, machinery, bombs and maps,
Altimeters and guns and charts,
Coffee, sandwiches, fleece-lined boots,
Bones and muscles and minds and hearts,
English saplings with English roots,
Deep in the earth they've left below.
Lie in the dark and let them go.
Lie in the dark and listen.

Lie in the dark and listen.
They're going over in waves and waves,
High above the villages, hills and streams,
Country churches and little graves,
And little citizens worried dreams.
Very soon they'll have reached the bays
And cliffs and sands where they used to be
Taken for summer holidays.
Lie in the dark and let them go.
Their's is a world we'll never know.
Lie in the dark and listen.

Lie in the dark and listen.
City magnates and steel contractors,
Factory workers and politicians,
Soft, hysterical little actors,
Ballet dancers, reserved musicians,
Safe in your warm, civilian beds,
Count your profits and count your sheep.
Life is passing above your heads.
Just turn over and try to sleep.
Lie in the dark and let them go.
There's one debt you'll forever owe.
Lie in the dark and listen.

The Collected Lyrics of Noel Coward

*by kind permission of Random House UK
Ltd from the 'Collected Verse' by Noel
Coward, published by Methuen*

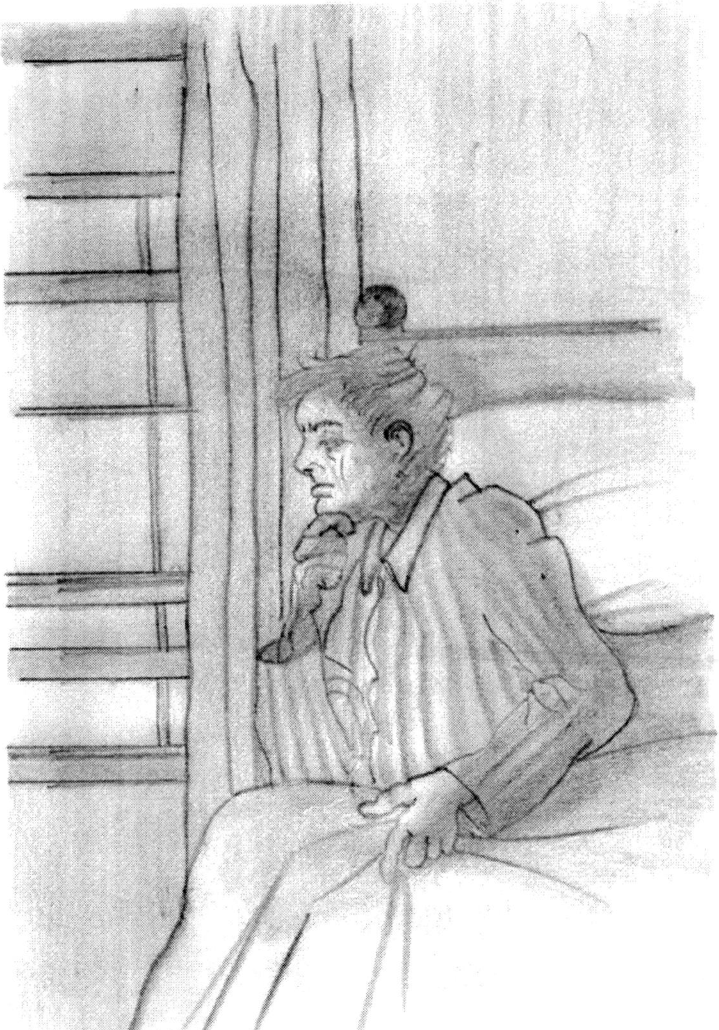

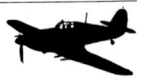

Acknowledgments

Since embarking on the formation of this anthology, I have experienced considerable co-operation and encouragement from many individuals, in particular those having had connections directly or indirectly with the Royal Air Force, also from various organisations and a number of publishing houses. In the very early days, I was fortunate in having a conversation with now late Wing Commander 'Laddie' Lucas CBE, DSO, DFC, RAF. He was most supportive of my aims, generously gave me the advice of his own publishing experiences, provided me with names of contacts and generally directed me along the correct flight-path.

My thanks to Air Vice Marshal David Scott-Malden DSO, DFC & Bar, RAF, who advised me on his translation of 'Epitaph' and 'Nesbyen Memorial', which will appear in a later edition, and for allowing me the use of 'After Battle'.

To Squadron Leader Tony Spooner DSO, DFC, Vice President Air Forces George Cross Island Association, my appreciation for allowing me to use the Coastal Command poetry written by himself. It is also as a result of Tony's consideration that he kindly introduced me to his relative Rosemary Anne Sisson the well known playwright, poet, film and television writer. She generously allowed me to select works from her repertoire resulting in the inclusion of 'Commonplace 1943' and 'Fighter Pilot's Wife'. Rosemary is President of the Writer's Guild of Great Britain and has been awarded the Laurel Award for Service to Writers.

I am grateful to John Snook for his encouragement and for permission to use his works of which 'Beaten Up On The Circuit' appears in this book. To Vicky Wallens who I thank for the use of 'The Fringe Of Glory' and the emotive 'The Last Scramble' by her late husband Squadron Leader 'Wally' Wallens. To Lady Balfour, who again in the early days of my research, responded with enthusiasm and allowed me the use of the late Lord Harold Balfour's poems 'Hurricane 1940' and 'Biggin Hill July 1947'. My thanks to Walter Scott for his touching tribute to a 'Showpiece - Lancaster'. Walter's poetry has brought him success Nationally and Internationally and has been recognised by 'The Poetry Institute of the British Isles'.

I would like to thank Victor Selwyn of 'The Salamander Oasis Trust' for answering numerous questions asked of 'The Trust', for permission to quote from and use poetry appearing in their own anthologies, for the benefit of his advice and for his enthusiastic encouragement of this anthology.

All of the following have contributed, in no less a way, with valuable help or permission for the use of poems that have been selected for this anthology and to them I am equally grateful:

The Commandant - Royal Air Force College Cranwell.
Ministry of Defence - Air Historical Branch (RAF)
RAF Innsworth - Personnel Management Centre
Royal Air Forces Association
Bomber Command Association
Commonwealth War Graves Commission
Lincolnshire Aviation Heritage Centre
Reading Room Staff - Imperial War Museum

The Poetry Library
The Poetry Society
Airlife Publishing Ltd.
Peter Waller - Ian Allan Publishing
Ken Delve - Fly Past
Ken Ellis - Midland Publishing Ltd
Hugh Cawdron - 578 Burn Association
Blackwell Publishers
This England Magazine
Everyman's Library
Johnathon Clifford - National Poetry Foundation
Bruce Robertson
William R. Chorley
Brenda Dunn
Don Neate

Last but not least, I am truly thankful to the Royal Air Force Benevolent Fund and to the publisher Bob Wilson of Wilbek & Lewbar, for having the faith in supporting this collection of stories that tell of war in the air. Also to Ted and Emma for their tasteful illustrations and layout

The poems in this book have been extracted from reference books, anthologies, magazines and newspapers. Some have been given to me and as can be seen, I have penned some feelings of my own. I have made every endeavour to contact all writers, their descendants where applicable, agents or publishers. In some cases this has not been possible because of the passage of time, a number having given their lives during the Second World War and others having passed away in the interim. Where some of the poems have been given to me, albeit the writer is known, it has been impossible to find a starting point to trace the source of ownership. A few enquiries have been returned as no longer known and some, mainly publishing firms have failed to reply. I regret therefore any omission but will be only too pleased to hear from anyone not credited, particularly if identification is possible of any of the 'Unknown 'writers. I hope it will be appreciated that the preparation of the book on my part, has not been for self recognition but primarily to present this poetry from some fine writers, in a publication it is hoped will make funds available for the welfare of former or serving members of the Royal Air Force.

A number of the poems have been used previously in anthologies with some appearing for the first time. This is not the first anthology of air force poetry and will not be the last but, I hope the combined collection, from the editions to be published, will be viewed as being some of the best that have been written and I hope the reader agrees with me.

Information

Other Poetry Titles Published:

Chants of the Spirits	ISBN 1 901284 00 X
Dreams of the Raven	ISBN 1 901284 01 8
Mystic Moods	ISBN 1 901284 02 6
The Spirit of Christmas	ISBN 1 901284 08 5
Circles of Love	ISBN 1 901284 03 4
Memories of a Wiltshire Farmer	ISBN 1 901284 04 2
Meditating Dreams	ISBN 1 901284 07 7
This Wonderful World	ISBN 1 901284 06 9
Life's a Laugh	ISBN 1 901284 09 3
Life's Little Miracles	ISBN 1 901284 10 7
Earth's Rhapsody	ISBN 1 901284 11 5

Coming out later this year :- Bombers Moon, Never Forgotten, Candlelight Visions.

If you would like to know more about our illustrated poetry books, then do contact us:

Wilbek & Lewbar
PO Box 1266
Devizes
Wiltshire
United Kingdom
SN10 1UF

Tel / Fax: 01380 720271
E-mail: wil.bar@zetnet.co.uk